A Pet

by Michèle Dufresne

Pioneer Valley Educational Press, Inc.

"I like birds," said Mom.

"Here is a bird."

Dad said, “I like turtles.
Here is a turtle.”

My friend said,

"I like dogs.

Here is a dog."

"Here is a rabbit,"

said Dad.

"I like rabbits."

My friend said,

"Here is a fish.

I like fish."

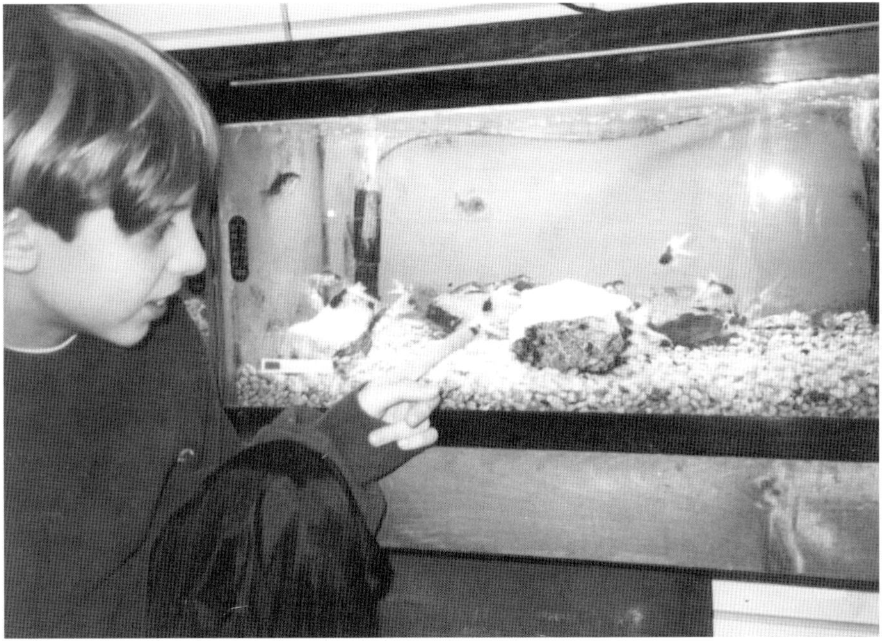

"Here is a mouse,"

said Mom.

"I like mice."

I said,

"Here is a snake.

I like snakes."

"No! No! No!"
said my mom and my dad
and my friend.